00033603

WITHDRAWN

658.85
YEU

DUMFRIES & GALLOWAY COLLEGE

Heathhall Dumfries DG1 3QZ • Tel. (01387) 243826 / 261261

LEARNING RESOURCES CENTRE

This book is due for return on or before date shown below

2 WEEK LOAN

D1380781

Time-saving books that teach specific skills to busy people, focusing on what really matters; the things that make a difference – the *essentials*.

Other books in the series include:

Preparing a Marketing Plan

Leading Teams

Making Meetings Work

The Ultimate Business Plan

Speak Out With Confidence

Writing Business E-mails

Buying a Franchised Business

Going for Self-Employment

Making Great Presentations

For full details please send for a free copy of the latest catalogue.
See back cover for address.

Anyone Can Sell

Rob Yeung

ESSENTIALS

Published in 2001 by
How To Books Ltd, 3 Newtec Place,
Magdalen Road, Oxford OX4 1RE, United Kingdom
Tel: (01865) 793806   Fax: (01865) 248780
email: info@howtobooks.co.uk
www.howtobooks.co.uk

All rights reserved. No part of this work may be reproduced or stored
in an information retrieval system (other than for purposes of review),
without the express permission of the publisher in writing.

© **Copyright 2001 How To Books Ltd**

British Library Cataloguing in Publication Data.
A catalogue record for this book is available from
the British Library.

Edited by Diana Brueton
Cover design by Shireen Nathoo Design
Produced for How To Books by Deer Park Productions
Typeset by PDQ Typesetting, Newcastle-under-Lyme, Staffordshire
Printed and bound in Great Britain by Bell & Bain Ltd., Glasgow

NOTE: The material contained in this book is set out in good faith for
general guidance and no liability can be accepted for loss or expense
incurred as a result of relying in particular circumstances on
statements made in the book. Laws and regulations are complex
and liable to change, and readers should check the current position
with the relevant authorities before making personal arrangements.

ESSENTIALS *is an imprint of*
How To Books

Contents

Preface

Every day thousands of people use selling skills without even realising it. Selling isn't just done by people with the word 'sales' in their job titles.

Anyone who is self-employed or works freelance needs to sell. In fact, anyone who wants to make a living from what they make or do needs selling skills. Whatever your product, skills or service – and whether you work for a company or for yourself – you need to find some way to connect with potential customers or clients who will pay you for those products, skills or services. This book shows you not only how to do it, but how to do it well. Or if you have been selling for some time, this book will give you new insight into how to really excel at what you do.

Selling is not about tricking or forcing customers into buying things that they never wanted. Instead, successful selling is about listening to customers, understanding their needs, and then helping them to make buying decisions that are right for them.

This book is aimed at people who want to learn how to build long-term relationships with customers. If your customers trust you, they recommend you to their friends and come back for more. This book shows you the essentials – what really matters – if you want to find a straightforward way to succeed in selling.

Rob Yeung

1 Getting Started

Dispelling the myths of selling is as important as learning the importance and skills of selling.

In this chapter, five things that really matter:
~ Understanding selling
~ Networking effectively
~ Clarifying your networking objectives
~ Preparing to talk to people
~ Setting up meetings

Who needs selling skills? The answer is anyone who has a product or service to offer to other people. Whether you have professional skills to offer your clients or tangible products that people can see, you need to find some way of promoting them.

Thankfully, selling is not about learning secret techniques or ways of tricking customers into buying from you. Succeeding at selling is about showing potential customers that you are **trustworthy** and have their best interests at heart – that you will only provide them with services that meet their needs.

It doesn't require cold calling either, as the most successful sales people **network** effectively – in other words, they meet people face-to-face and enjoy telling them about what skills or products they have to offer. It's a powerful tool that works.

It may be at a party or talking with other parents while waiting to pick your children up from school that you meet someone who is interested. Only then is it time to home in and **set up a more formal meeting** to see if your services can be put to good use.*

Is this you?

* *Selling doesn't have to be about aggressive pitches, deception, and cold calling. People are far more likely to buy from people that they trust to look after their best interests.*

• I'm not in sales – I'm just self-employed – so why do I need selling skills? • I've just quit my job and gone freelance – but how do I get clients now? • Even though I've been working in marketing for years, I want to learn a more effective way of getting customer orders in. • I have a product to sell,

but don't know where to start! • I have lots of
contacts who might be interested in what I've
got to offer, but don't know how to get the
discussion going. • My biggest worry is about
coming across as aggressive or pushy if I
need to sell. • Isn't selling just a case of
telling people what products or services you
have to offer? • I don't want to make cold
calls to customers – is there any other way of
promoting my services?

Understanding selling

Selling is a vital skill for everyone in business
– and not just for people in organisations
with the title 'salesperson'. Whether you're an
accountant or an interior designer, or just
want to make a little money selling
homecrafts in your spare time, you need
selling skills. After all:

~ How are you going to find the clients to
   pay for your financial advice?

~ Where are you going to find people who

will ask you to design their interiors for them?

~ Who is going to buy your homecrafts from you?

In other words, **everyone who has a product or service to promote will need to sell** to customers or clients of some sort.

Unfortunately, selling in the past has had a rather unsavoury reputation. The very word 'selling' brings up images of unscrupulous door-to-door salespeople who push their way into your homes and fast-talk you into signing on the dotted line for something you never wanted in the first place!

Thankfully, research has shown that the most successful salespeople are actually those who adopt a very much more personable approach. In the short-term a pushy salesperson might be able to persuade someone to buy something that they don't need – but the customer is unlikely to come back for more and will probably bad-mouth you to dozens of other potential customers.

Instead, the most successful salespeople

develop long-term relationships that are built on trust. If a customer trusts in you, he or she will come to you time and again – and even recommend you to their friends and colleagues.*

Networking effectively

Before you can start building relationships with customers, you have to meet them! Getting in front of potential customers is often the most difficult part of selling – but it doesn't have to be. Before we talk about what does work, let's talk about **what doesn't work**:

~ **Cold calling**. Although people often make 'cold calls', they simply don't work very well. You could end up making hundreds of cold calls before chancing upon someone who does need your services.

~ **Sending direct mail/mail shots**. Think about all of the 'junk mail' that you get. How many of these mail shots do you do something about? It's generally only large

* *Selling is not about pushing things on people – it's about building trust so that you can help people to decide to buy products or services that they need.*

organisations that can afford to send out hundreds or thousands of letters in the hope of getting one reply.

~ **Advertising in print, on radio or television**. While advertising can be useful, it can be very expensive! If you have the benefit of a very large budget behind you – perhaps provided by a large company that employs you – then it's fine. But if you're working alone or for a small company, it's better to avoid it for now.

What the above methods have in common is that they are like firing a scatter gun while blindfolded at a target. It doesn't take very much time, but you won't get a very good hit rate either. Instead, people who succeed at selling do so by **networking** – which is like aiming an arrow carefully for the centre of a bullseye.*

* *It takes more time to take aim and you can only go after one target at a time, but you're much more likely to hit the target and get some business in.*

Networking is simply a technique for **increasing the number of meetings you have with people** by using the contacts that you have.

Your first thought may be that you don't know anyone who might be interested in your services, but that doesn't matter. Even though your friends and acquaintances may not be interested in your services, they may know people who might be. And if they aren't interested, they might know people who might know people who might know . . . etc.

Start with pen and paper. Then **make a list of absolutely everyone you know**. Think about all the people you know in all the different spheres of your life, such as:

~ work life

~ past education

~ social life.

Don't just restrict the list to people with whom you are still in regular contact. There may be people you haven't seen for a few months or even a year or two who might be happy to hear from you.

And don't forget about:

~ Previous employers and your ex-employees.

~ Present or previous customers or clients.

~ Acquaintances through sports, voluntary associations, religious or political organisations.

~ People you've met through professional associations and institutes or conferences.

~ Suppliers, lawyers, auditors who you may have used in your current and previous jobs.

~ Family members.

It doesn't matter if your first draft of the list isn't complete. You can always come back to it and add more. And as you meet new people, your list will grow.*

* Networking creates an endless chain of prospective customers. In theory, every single person in the world is only six 'degrees of separation' away from you!

Clarifying your networking objectives

Given that your initial list may be dozens and dozens – or even hundreds and hundreds –

of names long, you can't afford to waste time when you are networking. If you try to talk to everyone on your list, you will quickly get swamped. So you need to **prioritise your list**. Divide a fresh sheet of paper into three columns with the headings:

~ useful

~ possible

~ probably not.

Then allocate all the names from your original list into one of the three columns, based on whether you think they may have information or access to other people who may be able to help you. Then start to get in touch with the 'useful' names first to avoid wasting time.

Before you start to get in touch with people, you have to think about *how* your contacts can help you. Only a minority of these people – if any – will be interested in your services. You certainly don't want to annoy them by pushing your services on them. However, you can ask for their help –

they can give you information or
introductions to other people:

~ **Asking for information**. First think about
the questions that you want to ask them.
Perhaps you want to find out about trends
in the market, for example, 'Is there more
demand for organically grown fruit in the
larger towns or the smaller villages?'
Perhaps the person on your list has run a
business of their own and could offer you
advice – 'You used to work as a freelance
writer, do you have any hints or tips on
how I could approach editors more
effectively?'

~ **Asking for introductions**. Although
information will help you out, it is
introductions that will eventually lead you
to customers.*

** Your time is
precious, so think
of who to speak
to and why you
want to speak to
them before you
make that call.*

Preparing to talk to people

If you network effectively someone will
eventually ask you 'what do you do?'

Answering the question is an opportunity for you to start the sales process. But you have to be careful not to talk for too long – otherwise you'll risk boring people!

So you need to think about a **'blurb'** – a short description of you and what you offer. Briefly, your blurb must include:

~ **A phrase or word that encapsulates your service**. For example, are you a 'management consultant' or a 'business adviser' or a 'business strategist'? Choose a phrase or word that other people will be able to understand easily.

~ **A brief description of the benefits that your service offers**. For example, a business adviser might help people put together business plans. However, the benefit is that his or her plans 'avoid the pitfalls that cause many people to go bust.' Similarly, a decorator decorates – but the benefit is that he or she 'saves you time and money by doing the job properly the first time round.'

You might also want to write out different versions of your blurb. For example, if you meet someone who is in a similar field of work you might want to include more technical details, whereas someone who knows nothing about your field might need a more generic blurb.

Then practise saying your blurbs out loud until you can repeat them without hesitation. Otherwise, imagine what a lost opportunity it would be if you were to find yourself tongue-tied while sitting on a train opposite Richard Branson!*

Setting up meetings

Now you're ready to get in touch with the people on your networking list. You may bump into some of these people over the course of your normal weekly activities. However, you may need to be more active by telephoning some of the people you don't see so regularly. Before calling, remember to:

~ **Relax** – take a deep breath and exhale.

* *Learn to talk about your work with passion. After all, would you want to listen to someone who was indifferent about their work?*

You want people to concentrate on what you are saying rather than having them wonder why you sound nervous!

~ **Smile** – as people can actually hear the difference in your tone over the telephone.

When you do get through to them, remember that these people are giving you something priceless in order to help you out – their time. So be careful not to abuse their time by trying to endlessly mine them for information or introductions as if they were a phone directory or a library. There has to be some give and take in your conversations with them by making sure that you:

~ **Show genuine interest in them** – start the conversation by asking what they are up to. Talk about the interests that you both have in common. If appropriate, ask about their family or work. Don't just go straight to the questions for which you are getting in touch.

~ **Phrase your request as a favour**. Rather

than demanding information or introductions, ask politely for them and remember that these people are helping you out.

~ **Offer to help**. After you have phrased your request for information or introductions, offer your assistance in any way that you can in reciprocation for their time.

For example: 'Actually, Steve, there was a reason for my call. At the moment I'm trying to find out whether people might need my services as a carpenter. Do you know anyone who might be interested at all? Or do you know anyone who might be able to help me find people who are interested? If you don't mind, could I take their number and give them a call?'

Eventually you will either meet or speak to someone who is interested in your services. At this point it would be very easy for you to recite at length all the exciting features of your product or all of the reasons why they should use your services.

However, it may be more appropriate (especially if you are speaking to someone over the telephone) to just give them your short blurb before setting up a more formal, face-to-face meeting. After all, there is a limit to how much trust you can build with a prospective customer over the telephone!

While networking is a proven technique for reaching potential customers, you must **be patient**! Networking takes time. You may have to call several times to catch them. Or it may not be appropriate to ask someone for introductions the first time you talk to them. It may take days for people to return your calls. And then they may not know anyone who is directly interested in your services. But don't give up!*

Summary points

* *Remember that someone will know someone who knows someone who does want to buy from you.*

★ Understand that the most successful salespeople in the world succeed because their customers trust them.

★ Don't think that you don't know anyone

who would want your services. Think about all the hundreds of people you have in your network and the hundreds of people that each of them has in their networks – someone is bound to be willing to pay for what you can do for them.

★ Spend your time carefully when networking. Start to get in touch with the people who you think are most likely to be able to help you.

★ Make sure that you know what your service is all about. Otherwise getting tongue-tied could lose you the chance of a lifetime!

★ Be patient and careful not to get on the nerves of the people in your network. Take your time to talk to them as human beings and not just sources of information. You don't want word to spread that you pester people.

2 Learning the Key Skills

Having a productive dialogue can't happen until the customer trusts that you have their best interests at heart.

In this chapter, five things that really matter:
~ Building trust
~ Asking opening questions
~ Exploring the customer's needs
~ Learning to listen
~ Reading customers

Customers don't like to feel that they are having products or services rammed down their throats. Meeting prospective customers and simply telling them about your services is an almost certain way to make them switch off!

In order for customers to feel that they are getting a good deal in buying from you, they need to feel that they **trust** that your services will provide them with what they need.

Being ready to ask **effective questions** will help you to explore a customer's situation. **Listening** to customers and learning to read their body language will help you to understand their needs. **Responding with empathy** and sincerity to their circumstances will make them feel comfortable telling you even more about themselves and their needs.

And when you have understood their needs, you will realise how best to position your services to help them meet their needs.*

Is this you?

• I don't really understand how you can get people to trust you. • When I meet people, should I talk about my services immediately? • I'm more used to telling people about my services than asking questions about their need. • What are the best questions to ask a prospective customer? • Should I take notes when I meet a customer for the first time? • I'd like to know how body language can be used to make customers feel more comfortable talking to me. • I'm not sure

* *Ask, ask, ask, then listen, listen, listen!*

what the difference is between an open and a closed question. • How can I tell if someone is really interested in my services or not?

Building trust

When you offer to provide your services to a potential customer, they have to **believe** that it will fulfil their needs. **Customers buy things for what they can do for them** rather than what the things are. They may, for example, want you to write a will for them – they want the feeling of security it provides them with. Or they may want to buy a home-knitted jumper from you rather than one from a high-street shop because they may believe that hand-knitted jumpers are better quality.

You need to get people to trust that your services will provide them with exactly what they need.*

In order to develop a rapport:

* *Building trust is about developing a rapport with your potential customer.*

~ You need to establish common ground with your potential customers.

~ You need to ask questions that will show that you are interested in their reasons for possibly wanting your services.

~ And you need to listen carefully to demonstrate that you understand what they are trying to get out of using your services.

Asking opening questions

Don't you find people who only talk about themselves boring? Similarly, people with services to promote who only talk about their services will usually turn their prospective customers off. Giving the customer a chance to talk shows that you don't fall into the stereotype of being a fast-talking salesperson.

You can't meet a potential customer for the first time and launch abruptly into questions about what they need. Customers hate being treated as customers! They want to be treated as people. After thanking them for making the time to see you, you need to start with questions that will help them to get used to talking to you. It's often a good idea to engage in 'chit-chat' on topics such as:

~ The weather – for example, 'isn't it cold today?'

~ Their journey – 'did you find your way here okay?'

~ The place you're meeting – 'I like your offices. How long have you been here?'

~ Their work or business – 'how are things going at work these days?'

If you have met the customer before – for example, if he or she is a friend or acquaintance of yours already – you could ask about the following as appropriate:

~ Their family – for example, 'how are Ian and David getting on at school?' or 'are you and your husband still looking to buy a new house?'

~ Other interests of theirs – 'do you still have

time to play squash these days?'*

Just think about what you talk about when you meet someone for the first time – you need at least a few minutes of general conversation before you can start delving into their needs. But although it's a good idea to have some questions at the ready, don't forget to be yourself! Customers are far more likely to buy from someone they like than someone who seems to be rattling off a list of rehearsed and standardised questions.

Exploring the customer's need

You need to get a good understanding of your customer's business, but do it in a way that he or she does not think is overly intrusive. Before asking searching questions to establish why they might be interested in your services, you need to ask for permission to question them. For example: 'Is it okay if I ask you some questions so that I understand your situation/business/circumstances/how I might be able to help you out?'

* *Make life easy for yourself – prepare five or six questions or common topics that you and your potential customer can have a chat about.*

Asking questions in a three-step logical progression will avoid making the customer feel under too much pressure:

Gather the facts

Start with questions of a very general or factual nature. The next chapter will give you some tips on how to prepare good questions to ask. For example, if they are looking for a new supplier to help their business, ask questions such as:

~ How many employees do you have?

~ What's the turnover of your business?

~ Who are your customers?

~ What exactly do you do for your customers?

These questions will help to build your understanding and start to get the customer used to talking openly about his or her situation.

Identify the need

Once you've gathered the facts you can move on to questions that try to examine the issue, problem, or need that has led to them agreeing to meet you. For instance:

~ What are the biggest problems you face in...?

~ What do you most hate about the suppliers you currently deal with...?

~ How satisfied are your customers with...?

Get the customer to weigh up the need

It's a lot easier to persuade a customer to use your services if they believe that they themselves came up with the reasons for using them. So help them to figure out why it would be worth tackling the problem or need that they have. The following questions might be useful in helping your customer to weigh up the consequences of taking action:

~ What do you think would happen if you

don't tackle these problems?

~ What do you think would be the benefits of having a supplier who could do that?

~ What would it be worth if we could make your customers more satisfied?

Once you have got the customer to weigh up the need and the consequences of *not* tackling the need, your services will seem like welcome relief to their problems.*

Learning to listen

Asking great questions is useless if you don't listen to the answers! But listening is not the same as just hearing something. Hearing is a passive process, whereas **listening is an active skill** that you have to work at.

Give the customer time to finish what he or she is saying. Interrupting customers as they speak or finishing their sentences for them will only irritate them.

Taking notes will help you to focus on what they are saying and serve to jog your

When you ask questions, remember to be polite and give your customers time to think – you aren't there to interrogate them!

memory after the meeting. In addition, it demonstrates to your customer that what they are talking about is sufficiently interesting and important for you to write down.

When you are listening, you need to use your body language to encourage your customer to keep talking. The following tips may also help you to demonstrate that you are listening and interested:

~ **Maintain eye contact**. If you do take notes, try to master the art of doing it without looking down. Keeping eye contact with people is a good way to show that you are interested in what they have to say. Looking at your notes could be misinterpreted by some customers as not being interested.

~ **Nod occasionally**. Nods of the head show that you either understand or agree with what the customer is saying.

~ **Make affirmatory noises**. Skilful conversationalists pepper their dialogue with words and phrases such as 'uh-um' or 'go on' and 'yes'. Most people do this naturally and it shows that they are following the gist of what is being said.

A good way to demonstrate that you are listening is to **summarise and reflect**. It also makes sure that you really do understand correctly. After your customer has finished explaining something, try to paraphrase what has just been said using phrases such as:

~ So it sounds as if ...

~ Putting it another way, would it be right to say that ...

~ Just to make sure that I understand you, can I repeat back to you what I think you seem to be saying ...*

* *But don't just repeat everything that a customer says like a parrot. If you don't understand something, don't be afraid to ask for clarification.*

Reading customers

While your customer's words will help you to understand his or her needs, there are often unspoken needs that you can read from their body language. Observing a customer's body language will also help you to realise how far you can take your questions and when to stop.

When reading body language, try to observe the following aspects of your customers:

~ posture

~ arm and leg position

~ facial expression

~ eye contact

~ breathing

~ gestures

~ voice quality.

For example, watching a customer's eyes will help you to spot when he or she starts to look at a clock on a wall or a watch on their wrist. If this is the case it may be that he or she is running out of time – so you should wrap up quickly! Or someone with their arms crossed and a cold expression on their face might be feeling defensive because they feel that your questions are a little intrusive.

Once you get used to observing customers' body language, you can start to **match their body language** as well. Matching body language is all part of the subtle ways in which people develop a rapport with each other. Luckily for you, it's a skill that can be learnt:

~ Start by watching people and learn to recognise natural rapport when you see others getting on well with each other.

~ You will often notice that they are both sat in similar positions, or have their legs or arms crossed at the same time.

~ They might smile, nod, shake their heads, or frown at the same time too.

You can learn to match too. For example, when a customer smiles, learn to mirror their expression back. Matching body language will help you to **demonstrate appropriate**

empathy with a customer's situation. For example, if a customer is telling you about a difficult problem that she is struggling with in her business, make sure that your body, face and tone of voice show concern for her situation too.*

Summary points

★ Understand that people who sell successfully do so because their customers trust them.

★ Learn to make polite conversation. Help your customers to 'warm up' and feel comfortable talking to you by asking them non-intrusive questions.

★ Begin to use more direct questions to unravel the customer's situation. Then get the customer to weigh up the consequences of not improving their situation.

★ Make sure that you use your body

* Reading and matching body language will help you to demonstrate empathy for your customers' situations.

language to demonstrate that you are listening to what your customer is talking about.

★ Watch your customer's body language to understand their unspoken needs. Observing their mannerisms and listening to their words will help you to build up a powerful picture of how to position your services most effectively.

3 Making a Good Impression

Thorough preparation lays the foundation for an effective first meeting.

In this chapter, five things that really matter:
~ Researching effectively
~ Warming up customers
~ Setting objectives
~ Preparing for sales meetings
~ Demonstrating customer sensitivity

Now that we've thought about the key skills in talking to customers, let's think about how you can make a great first impression. Customers can be quite wary of strangers – and this goes doubly for salespeople! You can really help yourself by **finding out** as much as you can about them in order to do what you can to **warm them up** before that first meeting.

Leaving a meeting with a confirmed sale is

a great feeling. But not all sales meetings are about getting a sale. Becoming successful at selling your services is about **building long-term relationships**, which can mean setting quite different objectives.

Making a good impression can depend on every single thing you do or show to a customer. So make sure you prepare well and manage the customer effectively from the moment you arrive on their doorstep.*

Is this you?

• To be honest, I don't understand the ins and outs of my customer's line of work! • I have to admit that I don't have a clue where to begin to research this customer's field of work. • I've only talked to my customer on the telephone so far, so I'm a bit nervous about meeting her in person. • Quite often customers don't buy my services straightaway when we first meet – does this mean that I've failed? • The customer said on the telephone that the meeting is just about getting to know me. But perhaps I should try some pressure techniques to make

* As little as a half-hour of preparation could make the difference between success or failure.

him sign on the dotted line. • There's always something I forget to take with me as I dash out of the door to meet the customer. • I don't have a business card. Do I need one? • Unfortunately I'm often late for meetings. Should I apologise to the customer or just ignore it?

Researching effectively

Customers like to talk to people who understand their needs and can ask sensible questions. They don't want to have to explain everything from scratch. Neither do they want to be asked questions that only poorly prepared people would ask.

Customers often talk in jargon or use phrases that are peculiar to their line of work and it's essential that you have at least a basic grasp of what they are going on about. Finding something out about the customers you plan to meet will also help you to feel more confident when you meet them.

There are two aspects to learning about your customer:

~ **Learning about their line of work**. It's important that you get to grips with the basic terminology of what your customer does for a living. For example, it might help you to write a brief glossary of jargon that you come across. Also think about recent developments or trends in their field of work. And try to figure out what problems people in their type of work may be experiencing at the moment. It will help you to ask the right questions.

~ **Learning about the individual(s)**. Customers are people, and people have personalities. In meetings some people like to get to the point, while other people like to ramble. Some people may hate flashy business cards while others may be impressed by them. Trying to find out something about the people you meet will help you to deal with their individual idiosyncrasies.*

* Appearing knowledgeable will help you to forge that vital rapport with the customer. After all, wouldn't you be impressed if someone had taken the time to find out something about you?

Good sources of information can include:

~ people you know who work in the same industry or line of business

~ annual reports

~ the Internet

~ books, magazines, or trade journals – you could get these from libraries or direct from trade associations

~ newspapers

~ People who have met or heard about your intended customer, such as acquaintances, ex-colleagues or suppliers of theirs.

Warming up customers

Meeting a 'cold' prospective customer should be avoided if at all possible. Finding different ways to interact with your customer before you ever meet will help you to sow the first seeds of rapport. So, when you do finally meet for the first time, your customers will almost feel that they know you and trust you.

Once you have done your research think of valid reasons to get in touch with your customer. The following list may provide you with a few ideas:

~ **Posting them a letter** (or sending an e-mail) confirming the time and date of your meeting. Perhaps you could add a few paragraphs in the letter about something that you have in common or reminding them about mutual acquaintances or how you got in touch with them.

~ **Telephoning** your customer to confirm that the time and date of your meeting still works for them. If appropriate, for example, you could ask, 'I wanted to check that 3.30pm on Friday is still good for you – because I know that this is a very busy month for you.' This shows your customer that you have their best interests at heart.

~ **Enclosing an article** on something relevant that you have seen in the newspapers recently. From your research you may know something that interests them – either from a business perspective or a personal point of view. And don't forget to mention in your covering letter how much you are looking forward to meeting them.

~ **Sending them a brochure** or any marketing information about your services. Alternatively, you could enclose a small sample of any product or physical materials that you use.

~ **Telephoning with a tip** or piece of advice that may help them out. For example, sometimes you can help one customer by putting them in touch with another customer of yours.*

* *Think laterally about ways of helping your customers out. After all, someone who 'scratches their back' is far more likely to 'scratch yours' and buy from you!*

Almost any contact you have with your customer before you meet will help to keep your name at the foremost of their minds. Giving 'free' advice to your customers demonstrates that you are **thoughtful and considerate of their needs** – in other words a million miles away from any 'pushy salesman' images they might have in their minds.

Setting objectives

It's important to establish objectives each time you meet a customer. Going into a meeting wanting 'to get the customer to buy as much from me as possible' is not a good objective, because it doesn't actually help you to formulate a strategy or evaluate how successful you've been.

Good objectives have to be **SMART**. This acronym says that your objectives should be:

~ **Specific**. Try to set out clearly what you intend to do. Don't always assume that you must secure a sale in order to have a successful meeting. Sometimes it may not be appropriate to get your customer to buy from you straightaway, for example if they are seeing other people with similar services. In such a case your objective might just be to 'get the customer to agree to let you prepare a written proposal for him.' Sometimes your objective may only be to get the customer to telephone you to set up a second meeting. Or perhaps your objective could just be to 'impress the customer with your professional attitude so that she will recommend you on to the people she knows.'

~ **Measurable**. You must be able to say categorically in the future whether you succeeded or not. For example, an objective to 'get my customer to call me' is measurable, whereas an objective to 'get my customer to like me' can't be quantified so easily.

~ **Achievable**. Whatever you propose must be within your means. In other words, you must be capable of achieving it. For instance, 'selling 400 units of your product' might be very impressive, but not very likely if you only have 200 units in stock!

~ **Realistic**. Whatever you propose must be within your customer's means. In other words, your objective must take into account the reality of your customer's situation. Aiming to 'sell £1 million of business' from your meeting may be out of reach if your customer only has a few thousand pounds to spend! Setting unrealistic objectives will just make you feel bad when you always fail to meet them.

~ **Timed**. You should aim to have an idea of how long it will take to accomplish your objective. For example, do you want to get your customer to 'call me within four days' or to 'call me within four months'?*

Preparing for sales meetings

It happens to all of us sometimes – that we rush out of the door only to forget something that we need for a meeting.

Help yourself to avoid having to arrive at your meeting without something you need.

Make a checklist of things that you need to do or take with you before a meeting. Then, moments before leaving for your meeting, tick items off.

Your list might include some of the following things:

* *Going through the thinking that is required to set a SMART objective will help you to plan tactics for how to achieve your objective.*

~ business cards

~ brochures, testimonials, or case studies

~ notepad and pens

~ charts, graphs, or other materials that you
   intend to show the customer

~ samples of any products that you have

~ your customer's address and telephone
   number in case you get lost or delayed
   and need to call ahead to warn your
   customer that you are going to be late.

You don't necessarily need a business card.
But you do need to be able to leave
something (eg headed notepaper, a brochure,
a hand-written compliments slip) with your
contact details on so that the customer can
get in touch with you quickly and easily.

   And don't forget to think about how you
will dress. You might want to wear a suit if
you are meeting a customer in a conservative
industry like investment banking or

accountancy. On the other hand, meeting a customer in the fashion business or someone who runs their own small business may warrant dressing less formally. Ten minutes of thought could make the difference between winning or losing the customer.

Demonstrating customer sensitivity

Customers do not want to be pushed into making decisions. However, understanding customers also means appreciating some of the other things that can annoy them.*

Here's a list of customer Dos and Don'ts:

~ **Don't be late**. If there's one thing that makes a bad impression it's being late. So leave yourself plenty of time to get to your meeting.

~ **Do check how much time your customer has**. Asking how much time your customer has for the meeting will show that you are sensitive to your customer's needs.

* *Step into your customers' shoes. Take just a few minutes to think about what might delight or annoy them – then act accordingly.*

~ **Don't interrupt**. Customers hate being talked over when they are explaining something. So do make sure that you listen and only speak when your customer has definitely finished speaking.

~ **Do be polite to secretaries and receptionists**. 'Gatekeepers' like secretaries and receptionists may not make the ultimate decision to buy your services, but they will almost certainly tell your prospective customer if you are rude to them at all.

~ **Don't ignore junior colleagues**. Your meeting may be with more than one person. Often there will be someone who is clearly more senior as well as someone who is more junior. However, don't disregard the junior person as they may have some influence on the more senior customer.

Summary points

★ Find out as much as you can about your customers and their needs. Having some knowledge about their businesses may just make the difference between choosing to buy from you rather than your competitor.

★ Get in touch with your customers as often as you can so that they feel they know you even before they've met you in person. Think about different ways of getting in touch with them – sending them materials, e-mailing them, or telephoning them. Almost any contact is better than no contact.

★ Take the time to formulate clear objectives. Specific, measurable, achievable, realistic, timed objectives will help you to plan how to deal effectively with your customer.

★ Avoid the embarrassment of turning up to a meeting without something you need. Make a list of things you must take with you and then tick them off as you leave for the meeting.

★   Think about actions that could make a positive or negative impact on your customers. Even the slightest negative impression could be enough to lose the chance to sell to a customer.

4 Presenting Your Services

It's time to explain to your customer exactly how your services will help them with their individual situation.

In this chapter, five things that really matter:
- ~ Understanding features and benefits
- ~ Explaining yourself clearly
- ~ Relating to the customer's needs
- ~ Writing proposals
- ~ Making a formal presentation

If you ask the right questions and listen carefully, you should be able to piece together a clear picture of your customers' needs. Only then is it time to talk about what you can do for them.

In order to persuade your customers to choose you rather than anyone else, you need to demonstrate that your services have **features and benefits** that meet each and every one of their needs. But it's easy to confuse customers with jargon or technical explanations. So make sure that you use plain English to make yourself understood.

Sometimes customers want more than just an informal discussion. They might need a written proposal to help decide whether to use your services or not. Or you might be asked to make a formal presentation to a group of customers. If so, make sure that you understand how to make the right impact every time.*

Is this you?

• I think I have so much to offer my potential customers, but I don't know how to convince them of it! • I know that I explain very clearly what services I offer, but customers don't seem that interested. • My profession is full of technical terms that I somehow need to explain to my clients. • I get frustrated because I know that my services are better than those of my competitors – but customers just don't seem to see it the way I do! • How can I convince my customer that

* Think about two vital questions in relation to each of your customers. What do you have to offer your customers? And why should they take up your services?

my services are exactly what he needs? • I find it quite difficult to write clearly, so I'm a bit worried about having to write this proposal. • I think I write good proposals, but customers just don't seem to respond very well to them. • The purchasing manager wants me to make a formal presentation to the board – help!

Understanding features and benefits

Having the most fantastic services in the world isn't worth anything unless you can convince your customers of the **benefits** of using your services. You really need to be able to differentiate between the features and benefits of your services.

~ **Features** are how you would describe your product or services. In order to map out the features of your service, think about the following questions: 'What is your service?' 'What elements make up your product or service?'

~ **Benefits** are what your products or services actually do for a customer. The key question here for you to answer for yourself about each feature is: 'Why does this feature help my customer out?'

For example, one feature of your service may be that you are a chartered or certified professional. However, you need to spell out the benefit of this to your customer – this means that you have guaranteed expertise over other people without the same qualification.

Or a feature of your product may be that it comes in different colours. But the benefit may be that the colour can match that of the customer's house or office.

Or imagine that a feature of your business is that you can deliver goods on any day of the week. The benefit to the customer is therefore that it will conveniently fit their schedules.*

* *Features describe to the customer 'what am I buying?' while benefits describe 'why should I buy it?'*

The following list of words and phrases may help you to think about the best **ways of describing the benefits** of the particular services that you provide:

~ Saves you time.

~ Is more cost-effective.

~ Is more relevant to your customers/clients/ readers.

~ Will be more convenient.

~ Is more comfortable.

~ Delivers results.

~ Lowers the risk of damage or breakage.

~ Requires no maintenance.

~ Wastes less energy.

Explaining yourself clearly

Customers hate being confused by jargon or technical explanations that they can't grasp. So you have to make sure that you speak a language that your customer can understand and connect with.

Avoid jargon

If your services involve technical terms, product names, or slang that is particular to your industry and not that of your customers – try to explain it in plain English.

Think about it – would you buy from someone who speaks the same language as you or someone who uses terminology that may seem unfamiliar? Rather than talking about the speed of the RS985 processing chip, you might want to explain about the shorter time that it will take your customer to load his computer files.

Use channels

There are also other ways of getting your point across. As you interact with your customers, you will notice that some of them may prefer to take in information in certain ways rather than others. You may come across people who like different **channels of communication**:

~ **Diagrams or pictures**. These people like to see pictures of the finished product, or diagrams that explain how the process of using your services will work. In order to sell effectively to these people, try to represent things as pictures for them and use coloured pens to illustrate how your services work.

~ **Written words**. Some people like to be given the time to read about your services. Selling to these people requires leaving them with brochures, case studies, testimonials and other written documents.

~ **Spoken words**. These people like to talk about things and to listen to words, music, and sounds that bring your services to life. In order to sell to them, try to use metaphors and evocative words to paint a picture in their minds. Or perhaps you could encourage them to talk to other customers of yours – perhaps over the telephone.

~ **To experience the service**. These people like to touch products or actually have a 'dry run' of your services. So selling to these people may need samples. Or you may need to give them a 'test drive' of your services.*

Relating to the customer's needs

To present a powerful case for buying your services, you have to **show that the benefits of your services meet each customer's specific needs**. Talking about benefits that do not relate to the customer's needs will make him or her start to question whether you are the right person to help them out at all.

For instance, it's all very well talking about how you can deliver a product within 24 hours, but it may be of absolutely no interest to a customer who isn't in a rush to receive it! As another example, think about how you might try to sell a car: a man who mentions that he has a young family might be more interested in the safety features of the car than its acceleration.

So that's why it's important for you to take notes as the customer talks to you about their particular situation. As they speak, try to

* Not everyone has a preferred channel of communication. But if you come across a customer who just doesn't seem to understand you, try varying your channel.

remember the key points of what they are looking for. And when it is time for you to talk about what you can offer your customer, you can refer back to each of the points. For example, you could say, 'you mentioned earlier that . . . ' and follow it up with the specific benefit of your services which relate to the point that they raised earlier.*

However, make sure that you are careful not to exaggerate what you can offer or 'bend the truth' at all. A deceived or unhappy customer will almost certainly spread the word and warn other potential customers not to touch you with a barge pole.

Writing proposals

Most customers will not make up their minds whether to use your services after only one meeting. Many will prefer to have something in writing to read and think about before getting back to you.

Proposals take many shapes and forms, but you won't go far wrong if you remember to

* *Customers buy because the benefits of a service match the needs that they are seeking to fulfil.*

include at least the following:

1. **Executive summary** – a brief overview of the entire proposal on no more than two pages.

2. **Customer situation, aims and objectives** – repeating back to the customer a brief summary of why they met with you and what they said they needed.

3. **Proposed method** – a step-by-step description of what you are proposing to do for the customer. This should also mention the timescales that you can work to. For example, can you deliver with one week or two months of notice?

4. **Investment/costs** for this piece of work – including a clear outline of exactly what is included or excluded for the price that you are quoting.

5. **References** – or testimonials or case studies if you think they are relevant.

Some sales people also like to include a few paragraphs on the history of their company or perhaps their qualifications.

6. **Appendices** – but only if necessary. If you are selling a specialist service, you might want to put all of the technical detail in here.*

You will also need a covering letter along with the proposal. A couple of useful phrases to pop into your letter include:

~ It was good to meet you the other day. Thank you for the opportunity to talk about how we could work together.

~ Please do get in touch if you have any questions or comments.

~ Once you have had the time to read and digest the information in this proposal, I'll give you a call in a week or so to discuss how we can best take this forward.

* *Above all, remember to write clearly. Use plain English at all times – no jargon or unfamiliar terminology!*

The last phrase gives yourself licence to get in touch with the customer, rather than waiting by the telephone for them to find the time to call. But just make sure that you do follow the proposal up with a call!

Making a formal presentation

If you are trying to get work with a larger company rather than an individual, you may be asked to 'pitch' to other decision makers within the organisation. Sometimes they may ask for a written proposal *and* a presentation!

There are three stages to think about for you to make a successful presentation:

Preparation

As a rule of thumb, you will need to spend about two to three times as long preparing your presentation as you will in giving it.*

* *If your presentation is going to be 45 minutes long, be ready to invest two or more hours in preparing your materials.*

Some of the things you may want to think about when preparing your presentation include:

~ **Purpose**. Why am I being asked to present? What do they need to know about my services or me? What are they still uncertain about?

~ **Audience**. Who is the audience? How senior are they? How many of them will there be?

~ **Timing**. How long will I have for the presentation? How long do I want to allow for questions?

~ **Content**. How much background will they need? What features and benefits do I need to get across in order to win over this customer? What are the key points that I want to leave with my audience?

~ **Logic**. Is there a clear sequence to the presentation? Does each section link clearly with the next?

~ **Tools and techniques**. What overhead transparencies should I take with me? What diagrams, charts, pictures or photographs can I use to liven up my presentation? Would a short video recording help get the point across? What handouts do I need to prepare? Do I need to use a flip chart and marker pens?

Rehearsal

Make sure that you do at least one complete run-through of your presentation.

~ **Check your timing**. Make sure that you finish within the time slot that the customer has given you.

~ **Get feedback**. If at all possible, rehearse in front of a colleague to get his or her ideas on how you could improve either the content or your delivery of the presentation.

~ **Familiarise yourself with your materials**. Order your materials and learn when to use a particular slide or overhead transparency and when to give out any handouts.

~ **Think about potential questions**. Once

you've done a trial run of your presentation, it may be easier for you to think of possible objections or questions that people may have. So prepare some answers for them!

Delivery

Some tips for making a good presentation:

~ **Breathe between sentences**. If you feel nervous when speaking in public, taking a pause to breathe between sentences will help you calm down and it will make you sound as if you are speaking more slowly.

~ **Project warmth**. Remember that customers buy from suppliers they like and trust. So make eye contact and smile at your audience. And let your sense of humour show – if appropriate.

~ **Vary your style**. Avoid speaking in a flat tone of voice. Try to vary the tone and volume of your voice to accentuate key points. Your hands can also be used to emphasise what you are saying. And use physical movement to keep people's eyes on you. Some people find it useful to alternate between sitting and standing while speaking.

~ **Leave enough time at the end for questions**. You don't want to leave people with lingering doubts, so make sure that you leave time and invite people to ask questions. 'That's all I have to say for the moment. Perhaps I could answer any of your questions now.'*

Summary points

★ Think about the features and benefits of your services. Why should someone use you over one of your competitors? Or why should anyone use your services at all?

★ Avoid using jargon or complicated technical language. Talk in plain English or risk confusing your customer!

★ Talk only about the features and benefits

* *Every single point you raise should be relevant to your customer's situation – so remember to relate everything in your presentation back to the customer's needs.*

of your services that relate to each particular customer's situation and needs. Information that is irrelevant to his or her specific situation will simply go in one ear and out of the other.

★ Write short proposals that only mention information that is directly relevant to that particular customer. If you're in doubt whether something is relevant or not, it probably isn't!

★ Allow plenty of time to prepare and rehearse your presentations. And when you do deliver your presentation, remember that people buy as much on who they see before them as what they see in the content of the presentation – so prepare well, but be yourself.

5 Negotiating to the Sale

Having impressed your customer with the benefits of your services, you now need to get their commitment to paying for them.

In this chapter, four things that really matter:
~ Handling doubts
~ Getting to an agreement
~ Walking away from a deal
~ Evaluating your performance

Customers may like what you've told them about your services, but it's natural for them to express doubts. In order to get the go-ahead from them, you will need to **deal with any reservations** that they have.

Once your customers decide that they want what you have to offer, don't be surprised if they want to negotiate a better deal. After all, everyone likes to feel that they've got value for money! So learn to be **flexible** and be prepared to **compromise**.

However, even the best salespeople in the world don't win over 100% of their customers. Luckily, lost customers are never a waste of time if you view them as long-term opportunities.*

Whether you manage to secure a particular customer or not, you should always **assess your performance**. Take the time to think about what you did well or badly. Only then will you continue to learn and become more successful at selling.

Is this you?

• My client isn't convinced that I can handle an order of this size – how can I convince him?
• The customer says that it's a big decision and wants to think about it. Is there anything I can do to win him over? • The customer wants 20% off and I'm afraid that she'll go elsewhere if I don't give it to her. • I desperately need to close this deal – how can I persuade them that I can do a good job? • I'm fairly certain that my services aren't what this customer needs. But

* *Getting a customer to invest money in your services is probably the most difficult part of the sales process.*

should I walk away from the contract? • The purchasing manager has ended up buying from our biggest competitor! What should we do? • The customer decided not to use my services and I'm not really sure why. • Several new customers have turned us down recently and I'm worried that we're doing something wrong – but what?

Handling doubts

Everyone is cautious about spending money, so it's natural for customers to have reservations, questions or objections about using your services. Perhaps they aren't sure about the quality of your previous work. Or perhaps they think one of your competitors could do a better job.

Whatever their reservations, you must be prepared to handle them professionally. The following three steps may help you:

Acknowledge the doubt

~ **Avoid jumping straight in with a denial**. For example if a customer says 'you're too expensive', jumping in to contradict them with 'no we're not!' will seem argumentative.

~ **Concede that the customer has a right to their point of view**. Agreeing with the customer that it is a point that needs consideration shows your willingness to listen. For example, to counter 'you're too expensive', you could reply 'yes, you could say that it's a significant investment.'

Resolve the doubt

Give your explanation for how your services are, in fact, right for the customer. There are two main ways you could do this:

~ **Accentuate the positive**. For example, 'it is a significant investment, but our service guarantees you that....' Or you could give them an example of how you have tackled it in the past.

~ **Give them proof**. Use the 3F formula of *feel, felt, found* to show how other customers had the same doubts but overcame them. For example, 'I understand that you *feel* that the price is high. Indeed, another customer also *felt* that the price was high. But in the end he *found* that the long-term cost savings that he gained from using our services were worth it.' Or, 'I understand that you *feel* that the software will be difficult to use. And in fact another customer also *felt* worried. But when she started to use it she *found* that our customer support team was able to answer all her questions for her.'*

Check that the doubt has been resolved

After making your explanation it's useful to check that the doubt really has been taken care of. For instance you could ask:

~ Does that answer your question for you?

~ Are you happy with that?

~ Have we dealt with that to your satisfaction now?

~ Does that help to alleviate your concern?

* *Put yourself into your customer's shoes, and empathise with their needs, to really help you understand their objections and how you could deal with them.*

Getting to an agreement

You may find that your explanations are not enough to tackle the customer's doubts. Sometimes you may find that you will need to compromise a little to win over the customer. But before you open up discussions about how you can be more flexible, it's worth taking a few minutes to think what you are willing to concede. For example, you may be willing to offer a discount of 20%. But what if a customer wants 30% off, or 40% or even 50% – will you give it to them?

Some areas where you could be more flexible include:

~ timing of delivery

~ size of order

~ discounting

~ terms of payment.

Even when you have offered customers a better deal, however, they often hesitate from making a final decision – 'I'd like to think about it.'

You can often hasten their decision in two easy steps:

~ **Agree with them** – 'Yes, it is an important decision.'

~ **Then check why they are hesitating** – 'But is there anything particular that you're still unsure about? Is there anything that I can clear up for you?'

The two-step process for dealing with hesitation won't be enough to convince every customer, but it will allow you to get at any final doubts if there are any and convince a greater proportion of customers than you would have done by just leaving them to think about it.*

Remember not to push your customers too hard though. Sometimes time to think is exactly what they need before coming back to buy from you.

Walking away from a deal

On rare occasions you may uncover in your discussions with a customer that your services can't actually do what the customer needs. Doing a bad job will give you such a bad reputation that the short-term gain of one customer will lose you many more customers in the future. So if you're sure that you can't do a good job, walk away:

~ **Explain to the customer** that you don't want to sell them something that is wrong for them.

~ **But keep in touch**. After your meeting, take notes on the customer – both on their business as well as their personal needs. It will help you to network with them more effectively in the future (have a look back at Chapter 1). Or if you see a new opportunity later on to sell to them, you can go back to them.

More frequently the customer may decide not to take you up on your services. Perhaps they decide that they just don't want to spend the money. Or maybe a different supplier can provide a better quality service. In such cases you may have no choice in walking away from the deal!

Whatever the reasons, don't let it get you down. As a rule of thumb, if you win over one in three customers you're doing an excellent job. One in four customers is still above average.*

With the customers that you do lose:

~ **Don't close any doors**. Accept with good grace that the customer doesn't want to use you. Don't badger the customer if they've made a final decision.

~ **Ask politely for feedback**. Ask for the reasons why the customer has decided not to use you – but again, if they don't give you any feedback, don't continue to hassle them.

* *Walking away from a customer takes guts. But you can rest assured that it will do your reputation as a responsible supplier a lot of good in the long-term.*

~ **But do keep in touch**. Again, keep records of the customer's personal and work needs. Perhaps three to four months down the line, you may want to give the customer a ring to see how they are getting on and whether the situation has changed at all.

Evaluating your performance

Once you've won or lost a particular customer, you must take the time to think about how you handled them. What lessons did you learn from your dealings with them?

If you didn't manage to capture the customer this time round, you need to consider whether there was anything you could have done better. And even if you did get the customer, you still need to ask yourself what it was that you did so that you can do it again with your next customer.

Take half an hour to sit down and evaluate your performance from the moment you first made contact with the customer to your very last contact with them:

~ What did you do well?

~ What did you do badly?

Accepting that everyone can always do better will help you to build a solid foundation of selling skills.

~ What would you do differently if you could do it all again?*

Some more specific questions you might want

to think about include:

~ How effectively did you **research** your customer and prepare for your first meeting?

~ Did you **greet** all the people that you met at the customer's premises – including receptionists, junior colleagues and secretaries?

~ Did you **listen** as effectively as you should have done? Were there any times that you interrupted your customer? And what effect did that have on your customer?

~ Did you feel that you built up **a good rapport** with your customer? If not, why not? What could you have done differently?

~ Were there any occasions when you didn't **explain yourself** as **clearly** and confidently as you would have liked?

~ How effectively did you **handle** any **concerns** that they raised?

~ How well did you **negotiate** towards a final agreement?

Summary points

★ Be prepared for your customer to raise objections! Try to empathise and show that you understand the customer's concerns before you explain how your services will tackle them.

★ Try to be flexible in how you will deliver your proposed services to the customer. Sometimes it's only a small change that will make the difference between winning or losing the customer at this stage.

★ Don't let it get you down if you don't manage to persuade the customer to use your services. Sometimes it's the right thing for both you and your customer. And remember that although things might not work out this time, the same customer could come back to you in the future.

★ Take a few minutes to assess how well you think you handled your customer. Really challenge yourself and think about everything you did. Could you have done a better job?

6 Building Long-Term Relationships

Making a single sale to a customer should hopefully be just the start of a beautiful relationship!

In this chapter, three things that really matter:
~ Looking after your customers
~ Evaluating your customer relationships
~ Completing the networking cycle

S elling doesn't stop when a customer has signed on the dotted line. After all, if they're dissatisfied they can always ask for their money back or gripe about you to other potential customers. So make sure that you not only deliver an exceptional service to them but also **make yourself useful** to them in all sorts of ways that will surprise them.

Sometimes a customer can take so much of your time and energy that you don't make any money out of them! You need to think about **who your best customers are** so that you can spend the majority of your time and effort on them.

Finally, a satisfied customer is the best source of recommendations for other potential customers. It's time to get networking again!*

Is this you?

• How can I develop repeat business with the same customer? • I want to sell a new idea to the same customer but don't know whether she'll go for it or not. • The customer was happy enough with his shipment, but I haven't spoken to him in the months since then. Is it too late to give him a ring? • I've heard of the concept of 'return on investment', but don't know how to apply it to the selling process. • I get so frustrated dealing with the procurement manager! I'm sure that he calls me twice a day and frankly I'm wondering if I really want him as a customer. • I hate networking! How can I get new customers without doing it? • I'm a bit

* Selling isn't a one-off event – it's a lengthy process. But if you are patient with it, you will learn to enjoy it and succeed at it.

reluctant to ask for recommendations. • Apart from providing me with new contacts, how else can my current customers help me?

Looking after your customers

You might have succeeded in selling one chunk of work to your customer, but the most successful salespeople recognise that it's easier to retain a current customer than to gain a new one.

In fact many large organisations find this part of the job so crucial that they call their salespeople 'account managers' – in other words, selling is as much about managing customers after you've gained them as getting them in the first place. After all, when you've spent all that time and energy gaining a customer, it would be a shame to waste it!*

* There is some truth in the old adage 'Out of sight, out of mind'. So work at staying in your customers' minds.

In order to keep at the forefront of your customers' minds, you need to:

~ **Establish a personal relationship with each customer**. Try to get to know them

on a personal – not just a work – level.
Keep track of notable dates in their lives to
show that you consider each customer as
an individual and not just a customer. For
example, if you know that a customer is
moving house, give them a call to suggest
a removal company that you know. And if
you find yourself in the vicinity of a
customer you haven't seen for a while, why
not phone them to see if they're free for
lunch/coffee or a drink?

~ **Act as a useful source of information**.
Invite your customers to call you at any
time if they ever need help or have any
questions that they can't answer. After all,
when you have lots of customers you will
be able to help your customers network
with each other.

~ **Keep an eye out for market
developments** such as news items or
articles in journals that you might come
across. If you see a press cutting that
seems relevant to a customer, cut it out
and send it to them. Helping them today

might help you tomorrow.

Evaluating your customer relationships

Not all customers are created equal! Unfortunately some customers require a lot more time and effort to get any money out of them. For example, one customer might buy very quickly from you after only a few meetings together. Another customer might require three or four meetings as well as a written proposal to convince them to spend the same amount of money with you as the first customer.

When you start to build up a number of customers it might help you to think about the **return on investment** (ROI) that you get from them. The ROI for each customer can be calculated as follows:

$$\frac{\text{Customer spend on your services}}{\text{Total time you invested in getting them to spend on you}}$$

This will give you a ratio for each of your

customers. Then you can compare your customers to each other.

You've probably heard of the **80:20** rule – sometimes also called the 'Pareto Principle'. It states that 80% of your business will come from only 20% of your customers. So once you've discovered the customers who generate the most business for you with the least time spent on them (i.e. those with the bigger ROI ratios), focus on those key customers.*

Completing the networking cycle

We already mentioned that people who succeed at selling are those who network effectively. The good news is that it gets easier when you have secured a few customers – because you can then start to network through your customers!

Once you have shown your customer that you can do a good job, follow the principles of networking to ask them for further contacts.

If you have a very good relationship with

* *Your time is a resource. So why invest your scarce resource in customers who don't repay that investment?*

any of your customers, you can also try to ask them to do something called '**customer get customer**'. If you've done a good job for a customer, you can try to turn him or her into a salesperson for you! Here's how:

~ Ask the customer whether he or she knows anyone who might be interested in the kinds of services that you offer.

~ Then ask whether your customer would be willing to call their contact to explain that you'll be giving them a call. Also ask your customer to tell their contact about the sorts of work that you have helped them with.

~ And then make that call, mentioning your customer. In this way you avoid having to make an entirely cold call.

~ Don't forget to ask your satisfied customers to provide you with case studies, references or testimonials. Politely ask them whether they would mind writing you a letter to add to your 'satisfied customer' file. In most cases they will be delighted to do so.*

Summary points

★ Make yourself indispensable to your customers. The more you can make yourself useful to them, the more loyal they will become to you – and the more they will buy from you and recommend you in the future.

★ Learn to recognise which of your customer relationships are likely to be the most profitable and prioritise your time to spend it with your most important customers. When you get busy you won't have the time to chase dozens of potential customers.

★ Don't forget to ask your customers for more contacts and to help you network. If you work hard to satisfy your current customers, then 'customer get customer' is one of the most effective ways of gaining more customers.

* *And so the sales process comes full circle, but each time you go round the sales process circle it gets easier. Good luck!*